A LOOK AT MONEY MATTERS

LOANS AND INTEREST

BY ROSIE BANKS

CRASHCOURSE

Gareth Stevens
PUBLISHING

Please visit our website, www.garethstevens.com. For a free color catalog of all our high-quality books, call toll free 1-800-542-2595 or fax 1-877-542-2596.

Library of Congress Cataloging-in-Publication Data

Names: Banks, Rosie, 1978- author.
Title: Loans and interest / Rosie Banks.
Description: New York : Gareth Stevens Publishing, [2024] | Series: A look at money matters | Includes index.
Identifiers: LCCN 2023031188 (print) | LCCN 2023031189 (ebook) | ISBN 9781538292341 (library binding) | ISBN 9781538292334 (paperback) | ISBN 9781538292358 (ebook)
Subjects: LCSH: Loans--Juvenile literature. | Interest--Juvenile literature.
Classification: LCC HG3701 .B26 2024 (print) | LCC HG3701 (ebook) | DDC 332.7--dc23/eng/20230711
LC record available at https://lccn.loc.gov/2023031188
LC ebook record available at https://lccn.loc.gov/202303118

First Edition

Published in 2024 by
Gareth Stevens Publishing
2544 Clinton Street
Buffalo, NY 14224

Copyright © 2024 Gareth Stevens Publishing

Designer: Leslie Taylor
Editor: Therese Shea

Photo credits: Cover (photo) Party people studio/Shutterstock.com; Cover & series art (background) creativenv/Shutterstock.com; series art (falling coins) Abscent Vector/Shutterstock.com, (moneybag) VectorArtist7/Shutterstock.com; p. 5 Freeograph/Shutterstock.com; p. 7 paulaphoto/Shutterstock.com; p. 9 Anton_AV/iStockphoto.com; p. 11 Prostock-studio/Shutterstock.com; p. 13 Rawpixel.com/Shutterstock.com; p. 15 Andrey_Popov/Shutterstock.com; p. 17 Doubletree Studio/Shutterstock.com; p. 19 89stocker/Shutterstock.com; p. 21 Efetova Anna/Shutterstock.com; p. 23 William Potter/Shutterstock.com; p. 25 Ann Baldwin/Shutterstock.com; p. 27 Krakenimages.com/Shutterstock.com; p. 29 marekuliasz/Shutterstock.com.

All rights reserved. No part of this book may be reproduced in any form without permission in writing from the publisher, except by a reviewer.

Printed in the United States of America

Some of the images in this book illustrate individuals who are models. The depictions do not imply actual situations or events.

CPSIA compliance information: Batch #CW24GS: For further information contact Gareth Stevens at 1-800-542-2595.

CONTENTS

Gift or Loan? 4
Borrowing Bigger 8
Asking Through an Application 12
Credit History 14
Shop Around 18
All About Interest Rates 20
Read the Small Print.........................24
What About Credit Cards? 26
It's in Your Interest 28
A Quick Look at Loans 30
Glossary 31
For More Information 32
Index...32

Words in the glossary appear in **bold** type the first time they are used in the text.

GIFT OR LOAN?

"Can I have some money?" You've likely asked someone this question. Maybe you needed quarters or a dollar to play a video game. Did the person give you money as a gift? Or did they tell you it's a loan?

MAKE THE GRADE

Whether you get an **allowance** or have a job, it's smart to make a **budget**. You can make sure you have money for needs and wants.

The difference between a gift and a loan is a big one! A gift of money doesn't need to be repaid. It's like any gift you might get. However, a loan is borrowed, which means it has to be paid back.

MAKE THE GRADE
If you're loaned money, make sure you pay it back. Ask the lender when they want it. It's good practice for the future!

BORROWING BIGGER

When friends or family lend money, they expect the loaned amount back. When someone takes out a loan from a bank or lending company, they're expected to pay back the full amount plus extra money. This extra money is called interest.

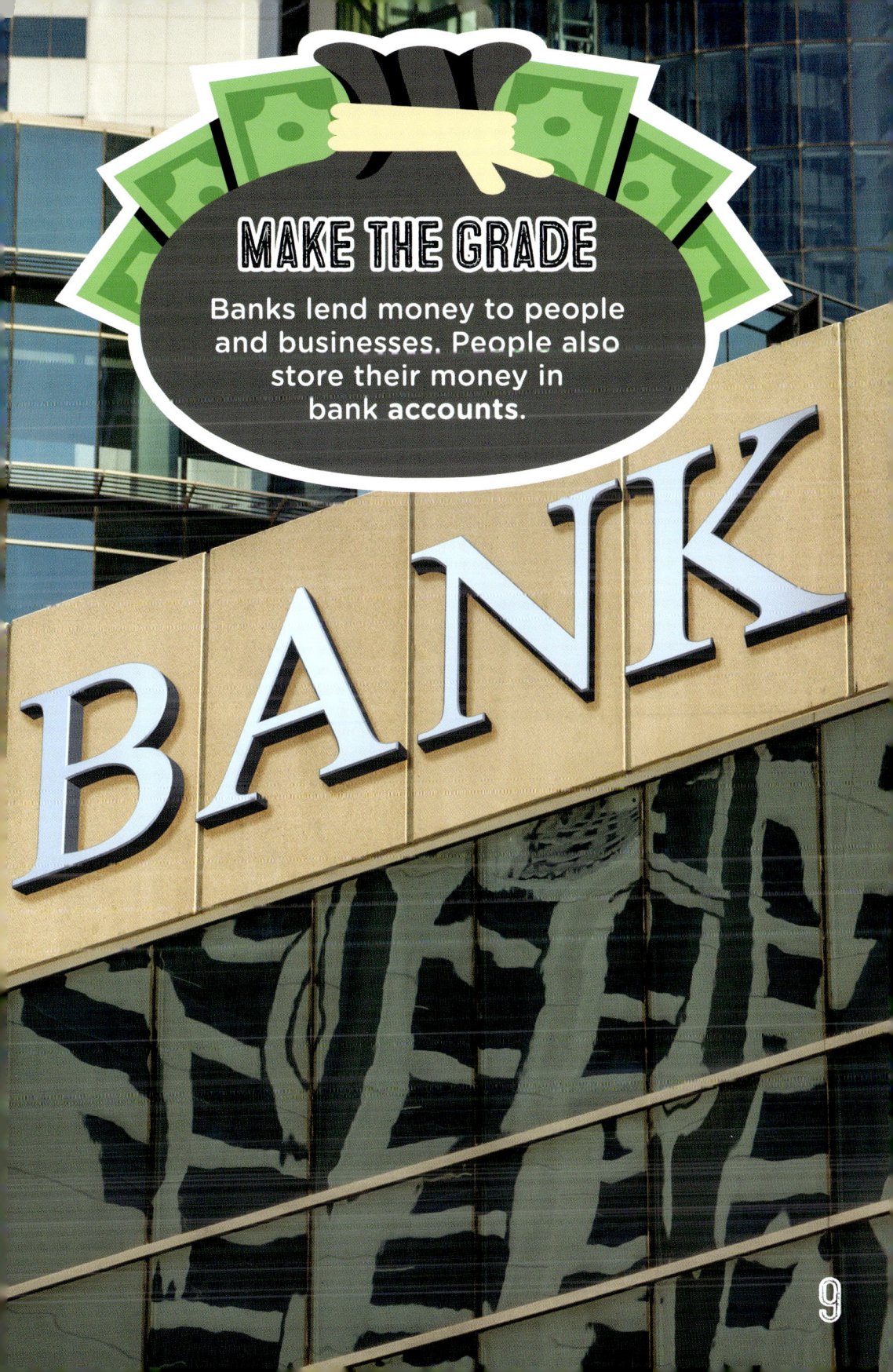

MAKE THE GRADE

Banks lend money to people and businesses. People also store their money in bank **accounts**.

People often need help buying expensive, or costly, things, such as homes and cars. A bank or company can lend money for these things. They **earn** money through the interest and other **fees** they charge to lend money.

MAKE THE GRADE

A person usually has to be at least 18 years old to get a loan from a bank or other lender.

ASKING THROUGH AN APPLICATION

Before someone gets a loan, they'll fill out papers or an online form called an application. On this, they'll tell the lender many facts about themselves. These include income, or how much money they make. The lender also wants to know about debt, or money owed.

MAKE THE GRADE

If you don't have income, you may not be **approved** for a loan. However, someone who does have an income can act as your co-borrower.

13

CREDIT HISTORY

A lender will check the borrower's credit history. This is the record of how someone has borrowed money and repaid it in the past. People who have always paid their past loans on time have a good credit score.

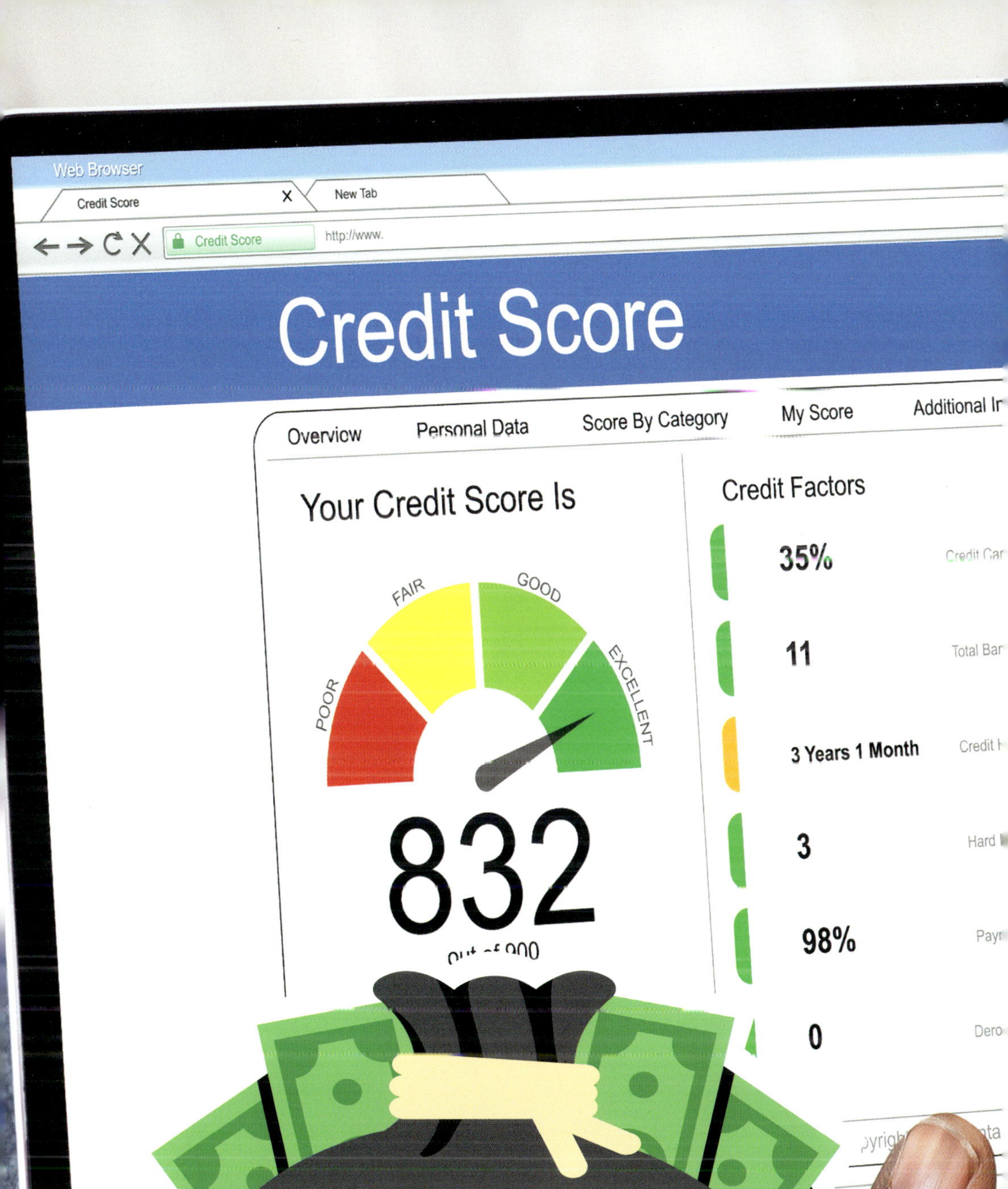

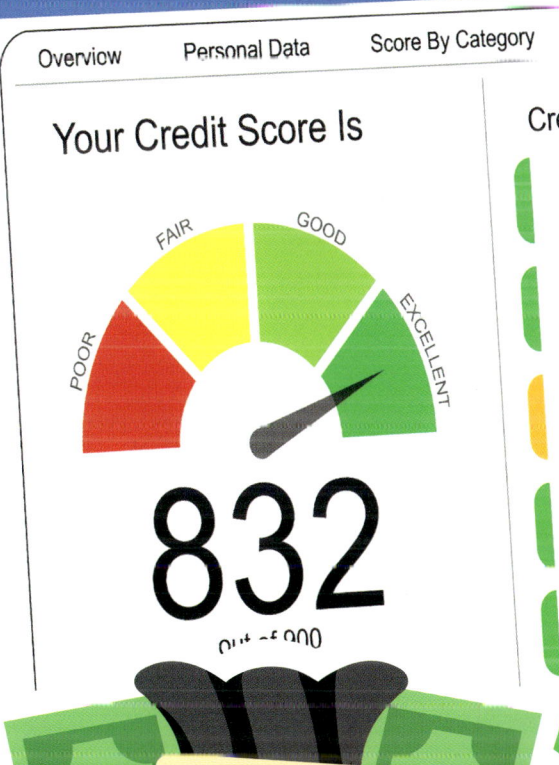

MAKE THE GRADE

A credit score is a number that tells lenders how likely you are to pay back a loan on time. A low credit score means you are less likely to. A high score means very likely.

A credit history helps a bank decide whether to give someone a loan. It also affects how much interest they'll pay. Lenders offer different interest rates on loans. The interest rate is the amount charged for borrowing. It's a **percentage** of the amount borrowed.

MAKE THE GRADE

Lenders are more likely to offer people with a good credit history lower interest rates. That means the borrower will pay less money to borrow.

INTEREST RATES
%

SHOP AROUND

People can shop around for a better interest rate. They can see what their bank will offer them. They can check out other lenders too. Interest can really add up for a big loan, such as a **mortgage**.

MAKE THE GRADE

A credit union does everything a bank does, but it's not-for-profit. That means the money earned goes back into the credit union. This can keep interest rates and other fees lower.

All About Interest Rates

Lenders have different kinds of interest rates. To find out how much a simple interest rate will cost, **multiply** the amount of the loan by the annual, or yearly, interest rate. Then multiply that answer by the number of years of the loan.

$100,000 (principal)
× .05 (5% interest rate)
─────────────────
$5,000
× 20 years (term)
─────────────────
$100,000 (interest owed)

$100,000 (principal)
+ $100,000 (interest)
─────────────────
$200,000 (total owed)

MAKE THE GRADE

The loan amount is called the principal. The length of the loan is called the term. In this example, the total amount the borrower will pay is $200,000. Interest adds up!

Compound interest is a different kind of interest. It's more costly. That's because the borrower pays interest on the principal *and* on the interest that collects over time. Interest can **accrue** by the day, month, or another time period.

MAKE THE GRADE

Auto (car) loans, **federal** student loans, and short-term personal loans often use simple interest. Credit cards and mortgages often use compound interest.

READ THE SMALL PRINT

When people take out loans, they must understand what kind of loan it is and how and when to pay it. Some loans require added fees for late payments, for example. Several missed payments in a row can mean the loan goes into **default**.

MAKE THE GRADE

A default is bad for a person's credit score. If the loan is for a car or a home, those things might be taken away. Income might be taken to pay off the loan too.

WHAT ABOUT CREDIT CARDS?

Credit cards work differently than other loans. If the amount charged, or borrowed, is paid by the monthly due date, no interest is due. However, if the amount isn't paid, the credit card company will often charge compound interest each day on the amount left.

MAKE THE GRADE

Credit cards can help you build a good credit score—if you pay them off! Use the card for needs, not wants. Make sure your income can cover the monthly bill.

IT'S IN YOUR INTEREST

Interest can make a loan hard to pay off. But interest can help you make money too! When you put money in a savings account, the bank pays *you* interest. You're earning interest so the bank can use your money for other people's loans.

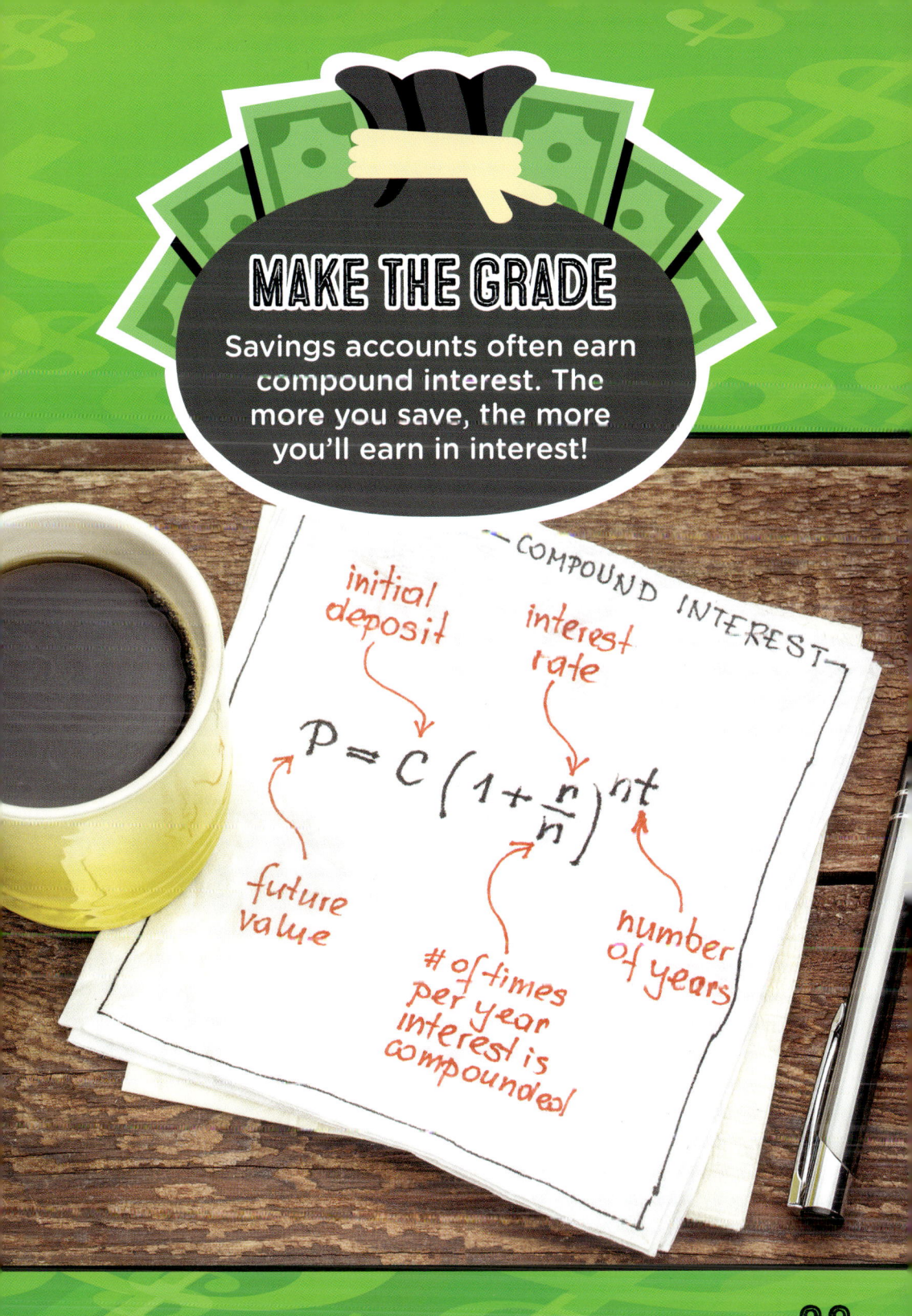

MAKE THE GRADE

Savings accounts often earn compound interest. The more you save, the more you'll earn in interest!

COMPOUND INTEREST

$$P = C\left(1 + \frac{r}{n}\right)^{nt}$$

- P = future value
- C = initial deposit
- r = interest rate
- n = # of times per year interest is compounded
- t = number of years

A QUICK LOOK AT LOANS

Mortgage
- long-term loan for home and property
- fixed (unchanging) or variable (changing) interest rate

Auto Loan
- short-term loan for car or other vehicle
- often fixed rate

Student Loan
- short- or long-term loan for school costs
- lower interest rates for federal loans

Personal Loan
- short-term loan for many purposes
- longer terms have higher interest rates

Small Business Loan
- short- or long-term loan for business needs
- fixed or variable interest rates

GLOSSARY

account: The money that a person keeps in a bank.

accrue: To grow in amount or value as time goes by.

allowance: An amount of money given to children by their parents.

approve: To give official agreement.

budget: To figure out how money will be spent according to a plan.

default: The failure to pay a debt.

earn: To get money for work done.

federal: Having to do with the national government.

fee: An amount of money paid for a service.

mortgage: An agreement bound by law in which a person borrows money to buy property (such as a house) and pays it back over a period of time with interest.

multiply: In math, to add a number to itself a number of times.

percentage: A number that is expressed as a part of 100, often using the % symbol after it.

FOR MORE INFORMATION

BOOKS

Gagne, Tammy. *Credit Cards and Loans*. San Diego, CA: BrightPoint Press, 2020.

Liu, Janet, and Melinda Liu. *What Banks Do with Money: Loans, Interest Rates and Investments*. New York, NY: Children's Press, 2024.

WEBSITE

What Is a Loan?
www.easypeasyfinance.com/borrowing-loan-for-kids-beginners
Check out this website created by a 13-year-old about loans and other money matters.

Publisher's note to educators and parents: Our editors have carefully reviewed these websites to ensure that they are suitable for students. Many websites change frequently, however, and we cannot guarantee that a site's future contents will continue to meet our high standards of quality and educational value. Be advised that students should be closely supervised whenever they access the internet.

INDEX

application, 12, 13
bank, 8, 9, 10, 16, 18, 19, 28
car loan, 23, 25, 30
credit card, 23, 26, 27
credit history, 14, 15, 16, 17, 27
credit union, 19
default, 24, 25
income, 12, 13, 25, 27
interest, 8, 10, 16, 17, 18, 19, 20, 21, 22, 23, 26, 28, 29, 30
mortgage, 18, 23, 25, 30
principal, 21, 22
repayment, 6, 8, 14, 15, 24, 25, 26
savings account, 28, 29
student loan, 23, 30
term 21, 30